IN THE ORCHARD

Anne Stevenson

In the Orchard
Poems with Birds

Etchings by Alan Turnbull

ENITHARMON PRESS

First published in 2016
by Enitharmon Press
10 Bury Place
London WC1A 2JL

www.enitharmon.co.uk

Distributed in the UK by
Central Books
99 Wallis Road
London E9 5LN

Distributed in the USA and Canada
by Independent Publishers Group
814 North Franklin Street
Chicago, IL 60610
USA
www.ipgbooks.com

ISBN: 978-1-910392-83-6

Enitharmon Press gratefully acknowledges the financial support of
Arts Council England, through Grants for the Arts.

British Library Cataloguing-in-Publication Data.
A catalogue record for this book is available
from the British Library.

Designed in Albertina by Libanus Press
and printed in Wales by
Gomer Press

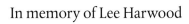

In memory of Lee Harwood

CONTENTS

INTRODUCTION

Almost my first memorable experience after I arrived in England from America in June 1954 was waking to the low, melodious voice of a bird singing in the apple trees outside my bedroom window. I was a guest in St Botolph's Rectory, Cambridge – later famed for its lodger-poets but at the time the home of the young man I planned to marry – and being full of Keats and literature after my recent graduation from the University of Michigan, I rushed excitedly into breakfast: Was it a nightingale? A nightingale? No, there had never been nightingales in the garden. Could I possibly have heard a blackbird? Vaguely I remembered an English nursery rhyme about a blackbird singing in a garden and thinking, even as a child, but blackbirds don't sing. True, in America, they don't. Obviously one of the aspects of England I was going to find enjoyable was getting to know its birds.

Sixty years of watching, looking up and identifying British birds have not turned me into a knowledgeable ornithologist; rather, birds have become so much a part of my life that they have occupied my poetry without my being aware. As I gathered poems for this collection I realised that I am not much interested, as a scientist would be, in birds' classification and distribution. Nor like a poet such as Wallace Stevens do I rejoice in an imaginative parading of colourful, exotic species. Instead, the same birds (so often blackbirds) appear again and again, seemingly because they connect for me again and again, sometimes with particular places or people, sometime with moods or ideas. In a sense, then, these poems are not *about* birds so much as they express feelings evoked by them. This is not to say, of course, that the birds celebrated here were not observed or acknowledged as real and wonderful creations of evolution, but that these poems at the same time celebrate human consciousness and its life-long imperative to look and love and praise.

ANNE STEVENSON
March 2015

THE ENIGMA

Falling to sleep last night in a deep crevasse
between one rough dream and another I seemed,
still awake, to be stranded on a stony path,
and there the familiar enigma presented itself
in the shape of a little trembling lamb.
It was lying like a pearl in the trough between
one Welsh slab and another, and it was crying.

I looked around, as anyone would, for its mother.
Nothing was there. What did I know about lambs?
Should I pick it up? Carry it . . . where?
What would I do if it were dying? The hand
of my conscience fought with the claw of my fear.
It wasn't so easy to imitate The Good Shepherd
in that faded, framed Sunday school picture
filtering now through the dream's daguerreotype.

With the wind fallen and the moon swollen to the full,
small, white doubles of the creature at my feet
flared like candles in the creases of the night
until it looked to be alive with new-born lambs.
Where could they all have come from?
A second look, and the bleating lambs were birds –
kittiwakes nesting, clustered on a cliff face,
fixing on me their dark accusing eyes.

There was a kind of imperative not to touch them,
yet to be of them, whatever they were –
now lambs, now birds, now floating points of light –
fireflies signalling how many lost New England summers?
One form, now another; one configuration, now another.
Like fossils locked deep in the folds of my brain,
outliving a time by telling its story. Like stars.

IN THE ORCHARD

Black bird, black voice,
almost the shadow of a voice,
so kind to this tired summer sky,
a rim of night around it,
almost an echo of today,
all the days since that first
soft guttural disaster
gave us 'apple' and 'tree'
and all that transpired thereafter
in the city of the tongue.

Blackbird, so old, so young, still
happy to be stricken with a song
you can never choose away from.

SISKIN

Glasgow, 1967, remembering my mother

Small bird with green plumage,
yellow to green to white
on the underparts, yes, a siskin
alive on my own cedar,
winter visitor, resident in Scotland,
wholly himself.

I saw him, and you, too,
alive again,
thin but expert, seated
with your bird glasses, bird book
and concentrated expression,
hoping for siskins in Vermont.

He pleased me for your sake –
not so much as he would have pleased you.
Unless it was you he came for,
and I something you inhabited
from the second his green flame
flickered in that black tree
to the next second when he was gone.

RESURRECTION

Surprised by spring,
by a green light fallen like snow
in a single evening –
blackthorn, hawthorn, willow,
meadow – everything
woken again after how many million years?

That generous throat
is a blackbird's. Now a thrush.
And that ribbon flung out,
that silk voice, is a chaffinch's rush
to his grace-note. Birds woo
or apportion the innocent air they're made for.
Whom do they sing for?

Old man by the river –
spread out like a cross in the sun,
feet bare and stared at
by three grubby children – you've made it again,
and, yes, we'll inherit a summer.
Always the same green clamouring fells you that wakes you.
And you have to start living again when it wakes you.

BIRD IN HAND

The tiny wren perched on your hand
could be a key. Then
somewhere should be the door
that with a bird-shaped key-hole
cut by wind into stiff sand
must fit that needle beak and pinhead eye,
that tail's armed signal to the clamped wings,
Fly! Spring the lock! Lift the floor
from the earth, the roof from the sky,
and with a fanfare of trills
– no trumpets, no veils –
reveal the Quaker heaven where this bird sings.

SWIFTS

Spring comes little, a little. All April, it rains.
The new leaves stick in their fists; new ferns still fiddleheads.
But one day the swifts are back. Face to the sun like a child
You shout, 'The swifts are back!'

Sure enough, bolt knocks bow to carry one sky-scyther
Two hundred miles an hour across fullblown windfields.
Swereee, swereee. Another. And another.
It's the cut air falling in shrieks on our chimneys and roofs.

The next day a fleet of high crosses cruises in ether.
These are the air pilgrims, pilots of air rivers.
A shift of wing, and they're earth-skimmers, daggers
Skilful in guiding the throw of themselves away from themselves.

Quick flutter, a scimitar upsweep, out of danger of touch.
For earth is forbidden to them, water's forbidden to them,
All air and fire, little owlish ascetics, they outfly storms,
They rush to the pillars of altitude, the thermal fountains.

Here is a legend of swifts, a parable –
When the Great Raven bent over earth to create the birds,
The swifts were ungrateful. They were small muddy things
Like shoes, with long legs and short wings,

So they took themselves off to the mountains to sulk.
And they stayed there. 'Well,' said the Raven, after years of this,
'I will give you the sky. You can have the whole sky
On condition that you give up rest.'

'Yes, yes,' screamed the swifts, 'We abhor rest.
We detest the filth of growth, the sweat of sleep,
Soft nests in the wet fields, slimehold of worms.
Let us be free, be air!'

So the Raven took their legs and bound them into their bodies.
He bent their wings like boomerangs, honed them like knives.
He streamlined their feathers and stripped them of velvet.
Then he released them, *Never to Return*

Inscribed on their feet and wings. And so
We have swifts, though in reality, not parables but
Bolts in the world's need: swift
Swifts, not in punishment, not in ecstasy, simply

Sleepers over oceans in the mill of the world's breathing.
The grace to say they live in another firmament.
A way to say the miracle will not occur,
And watch the miracle.

SHARED

April at last, with me on my knees
digging roots out of broken soil – why
when a robin darts in, freezes me with an eye
and pulls a meal from my trowel,
do I feel so honoured?

TERRORIST

One morning I despaired of writing more,
            never any more,
when a swallow swooped in, around and out
            the open door,
then in again and batlike to the window
            against which,
beating itself, a suicide in jail,
            he now and then collapsed into
his midnight iridescent combat suit,
            beautiful white markings on the tail.

Inside his balaclava, all he knew
            was something light and airy he had come from
flattened into something hard and blue.
            Thank God for all those drafts I used to
scoop, shove or shovel him to the transom,
            open just enough to let him through.

Off he flew, writing his easy looped
            imaginary line.
No sign of his adventure left behind
            but my surprise
and his – not fright, though he had
            frightened me, those two
bright high-tech bullets called his eyes.
            What they said was
               'Fight and fight and fight. No compromise.'

PITY THE BIRDS

For Charles Elvin who said 'Poetry should protest!'

Pity
the persistent clamour of a song thrush
I can't see,
the gull's vacant wail, its sea-saw
yodel of injury,
that black and white wagtail bobbing
for a meal of midges,
rapacious Mrs Blackbird shopping on foot
in the hedges,
yesterday's warbler, lying stiff on the step
to the barn,
olive green wings torn awry by the wind,
eyes gone,
but with tri-clawed reptilian feet still
hungrily curled.

Not one of them gened to protest
against the world.

PHOENICURUS PHOENICURUS

Phu-eet! Phu-eet! Mr unresting redstart has something to be
anxious about. A nest of eggs? Babies? Or has he
lost them already to the weasel scared away yesterday,

slithering (guilty? sinister?) out of a rock hole?
Phu-eet, on and on, a tiny uptilted, not really hysterical
shriek. Greeting his mate on top of the clothes pole . . .

gone. Divers? No, rust-tinted streamers, each, so to speak,
with an end of invisible raffia in its beak.
So where is the camouflaged nook or lichenous crack

that has to be wicker-worked, netted inside those flights?
Such showy displays and flash, panic-coloured lights!
Calm down, pretty bird! You've been gulping big bites

from my reading and writing all morning. Stay still!
What wars do you have to survive, with your phoenix tail,
in all that Darwinian weather, too small, too frail?

Snug in my nest of vocabularies, safe in my view,
I've had to jump up three, four times, just to
tell Something Awful out there to be careful of you.

Phu-eet, a more and more panicky piping, *phu-eet!*
And not meaning anything I mean. In the grammar of tweet
why did we ever say birds should sound *sweet, sweet?*

THE BLACKBIRD AT PWLLYMARCH

After the ninth-century Irish lyric, 'The Blackbird at Belfast Lough'

For Stephen Regan

Because I live here
I have learned from the gorsebush
how to whistle yellow petals
out of my bright beak,

though I can remember
wooded fells loud with waterfalls
and curlews crying in the marsh
that was once a lake.

FROM 'SPRING DIARY'
North Wales

A CLEARER MEMORY

Every spring renews the blackbird for me
just when he claims the season for himself,
as out of the deep well of his voice I heft,
with a longer rope, a clearer memory.

      Then, like a present,

two weeks of dry wind – joy for the jackdaws –
sweeping the air with haze and chaffinches.
The old house complains . . . those aching doors.
Mud becomes dust in the ditches.
Summer has locked up its hostile barometers.
Light cleans protesting corners with dirty fingers.

GANNETS DIVING

The sea is dark
by virtue of its white lips;
the gannets white
by virtue of their dark wings.

Gannet into sea.

Cross the white bolt
with the dark bride.

Act of your name, Lord,
though it does not appear so
to you in the speared fish.

CAROL OF THE BIRDS

Feet that could be clawed, but are not . . .
Arms that might have flown, but did not . . .
No one said, 'Let there be angels' but the birds,

Whose choirs fling alleluias over the sea,
Herring gulls, black backs carolling raucously,
While cormorants dry their wings on a rocky stable.

Plovers that stoop to sanctify the land
And scoop small roundy mangers in the sand,
Swaddle a saviour each in a speckled shell.

A chaffinchy fife unreeling in the marsh
Accompanies a solo trumpet thrush,
Half sings, half talks in riffs of wordless words,

As hymns flare up from tiny muscled throats,
Robins and hidden wrens, whose shiny notes
Tinsel the precincts of the winter sun.

What loftier organ than these pipes of beech,
Pillars resounding with the jackdaws' speech,
And poplars swayed with light like shaken bells?

Wings that could be hands but are not . . .
Cries that might be pleas yet cannot
Question or disinvent the stalker's gun,

Be your own hammerbeam angels in the air
Before in the maze of space you disappear,
Stilled by our dazzling anthrocentric mills.

CROW OMEN
(*Goat Cull in Cwm Nantcol*)

You, Mr Crow,
where are you flying to,
over the tawny marsh,
over the craggy fell?
Why is your voice so harsh,
casting your spell,
casting your hungry spell?
Mr Crow, don't call on me.

You, little goat,
where has your mammy gone?
Yesterday I spied a man.
He was a stranger on your hill,
stalking with his clever gun
and itch to kill.
Run, little goat, when you spy me, run!
That man was me.

FROM 'GREEN MOUNTAIN, BLACK MOUNTAIN'
Hay on Wye, 1980

PART VI

In dread of the black mountain,
Gratitude for the green mountain;
In dread of the green mountain,
Gratitude for the black mountain.

In dread of the fallen lintel and the ghosted hearth,
       gratitude for the green mountain;
In dread of the whining missile and the jet's chalk,
       gratitude for the black mountain.

In dread of the titled thief, thigh-deep in his name,
       gratitude for the green mountain;
In dread of the neon street to the armed moon,
       gratitude for the black mountain.

In dread of the gilded Bible and the rod-cut hand,
       gratitude for the green mountain;
In dread of the falling towers behind the blazing man,
       gratitude for the black mountain.

In dread of my shadow on the Green Mountain,
Gratitude for this April of the Black Mountain,
As the grass fountains out of its packed roots
And a thrush repeats the repertoire of his threats:

      I hate it, I hate it, I hate it.
          Go away. Go away.
      I will not, I will not, I will not.
          Come again. Come again.

Swifts twist on the syllables of the wind currents.

Blackbirds are the cellos of the deep farms.

BUZZARD AND ALDER

Buzzard that folds itself into and becomes nude
alder; alder that insensibly becomes bird –
one life inside the dazzling tree. Together
they do change everything, and forever.

You think, because no news is said here,
not. But rain's rained weather to a rare
blue, so you can see the thinness of it,
I mean the layer they live in, flying in it

breaking through it, minute by glass minute.
Buzzard, hunched in disuse before it
shatters winter, wheeling after food.
Alder, silently glazing us, the dead.

THE BULLY THRUSH (*TURDUS PHILOMELOS*)

Spring opens the air and lifts out the thrush's jeer.
   Aggression must be fixed in his genes like sex,
his instinct roused to possess, to propagate, to declare
until the beeches are his, their light green ranks
   unfurling in wrinkled flags, the apple blossom his,
that short-lived frivolity. Slaves of the system,
bees in striped prison uniforms, trained to ignore
   announcements of approaching holocaust,
perform, door to door, hungry acts of insemination.

'His song is flute-like', so the bird guide says,
   'short riffs or phrases, tending to repetition.'
(Flute-like? A sergeant major barking out threats and abuses,
a dictator in his prime, defending his ways.) Again,
that raucous, anxious, too insistent, *Have you heard?*
   Have you heard? Listen to me, listen to me!
Brag, brag, brag, brag! Halt die Klappe, Herr Drossel.
Let's hear instead the *molto espressivo* of the blackbird,
the chaffinch's A flat major Impromptu flung to the world.

Birdsong. Mysterious. And heard without words,
   more mysterious – the Word made wings
and other things, but not for you, or you and me
the song thrush sings. Blame it all on the birds,
   the myths advise, though they can't agree
which girl was which in those fabled happenings.
Was it the nightingale, raped and stripped of her tongue?
   Or was Procne the swallow, crazed by that atrocity?
I can't help setting a libretto to the thrush's song.

Every morning, fitting fresh words to his clamour,
lifting myself awake from half sleep or a dream,
I feel an old story pulling itself up from under,
   lending its meaning to codes in a mystery play

that for buried, uncountable years has been the same.
Untranslatable language with nothing to say,
give me a line for a poem. Write me a play.
  There's a plea, *don't leave me, don't leave me!*
Now fainter, *jug, jug, jug, jug, tereu* ... farther away.

CONSTABLE CLOUDS AND A KESTREL'S FEATHER

England still moulds them as Constable saw them.
We see them through his eyes –
loaves fresh kneaded for the oven,
veils of gauze,
flat-bottomed continents, creamy islands
floating on glass. As a child
did you never play the cloud-zoo game
on summer days like these?
Lie prone on grass,
stalk in your mouth, face to the sun,
to let imagination run wild
in a sky full of camels and whales
where the air-show today
features fish evolving into crocodiles
disintegrating slowly
into little puffs of sheep grazing on air.
Now a tyrannosaur, chasing a bear . . .
or is it a white bull? Europa on his back,
panicking to disappear . . .

Here's a cloud that Constable never knew.
Two chalk-white furrows are being ploughed
straight as rails across the high blue
hinterland of my childhood zoo –
a plane from somewhere, going somewhere,
leaving its spoor of vapour on the air.
As the trailing furrows widen,
waves form a lingering wake from a prow
in perfect rhythm, like a feather's pattern.

And still you keep your head down,
eyes vacuuming the turf,
nose to the ground,
intent on ants and other centaurs

in their dragon world, their home
here thatched with a found
feather – evidence of hunger's habits
in this summer field.
A kestrel's, female you guess,
stroking the patterned vanes
locked to the shaft:
13 square bars, dark, on the outer side;
13 wavy lines, woven on the inner side,
a russet, bow-shaped, undesigned design
perfectly aligned – not by craft,
but by a mathematics of its own –
proof that, undeterred by our millennium,
nature's nature is to work in form.

WINTER IDYLL FROM MY BACK WINDOW

Remembering Jon Silkin's Peaceable Kingdom, 2015

Naked and equal in their winter sleep,
Poplars, ashes, maples, beeches sweep
A bruised agitated sky with skeletons.
Not a leaf. Not a leaf. Lovely generations
Are shrivelling to mulch and mulchiness
Under highway flyovers and underpasses;
A race of acrobatic rats is
Taking place in the bone yard.

Shady rats, showy tails. Is there sex or food
Up there, where bloated pigeons brood,
Silent in wintertime, and Nazi magpies forage
Between raids? Cheeky greys! You manage
Too well, with greed and chutzpah, to keep
Your species lively, running pell-mell to leap
Four times your length, branch to scrawny branch . . .
! No, you don't crash.

For me, you're jokers in the trees;
For my bird-watching neighbour, enemies,
Though the tits don't seem to mind you
Guzzling from their feeder. The jackdaws, too,
Flap down in a noisy crowd, not noticing.
I don't get any sense that they're competing.
Perhaps these species never think of war,
Not knowing what words are for.

ELEGY: IN COHERENT LIGHT

In memory of Matt Simpson and Michael Murphy

Teach-cheap, teach-cheap, teach-cheap, teach-cheap –
Sparrows – plying their chisels in the summer ivy,
Chipping the seconds spark by spark out of the hours.
Each whistling chip repeats the sun's holography.
My brain's a film, I'm made of timed exposures.
Pounding my eyes and ears with waves of light,
Invisible flakes make pictures I call sight.

But now you're out of the picture, no one can keep
Coherent track of you, except in language.
All the warm rhetoric is wrong. Death isn't sleep.
Faith in eternal love is love's indulgence.
I prize what you wrote, meet you in what I write,
Still keep house in our crumbling tenement of words.
Pull down their walls of ivy, and you kill the birds.

STONE MILK

A backward May, with all the finches of the Fex Tal
      piping in dialect.
Grüezi to the nun-white finger-high crocuses
      thinly nursing to life the flattened fields.
Grüezi to the fisted bristles colouring the larches
      a green to break your heart.
The fairy tale resorts, scrubbed clean but closed
      because the coach crowds haven't arrived yet,
Look to be hospitals for convalescent ideals.

Imagine a breath held long before history happened,
Allowing a lake to drown its Jurassic memory
      in Elysian blue.
Conceive of the gentians' daytime midnight 'smoking
      torch-like out of Pluto's gloom',
Eden's anemones lifting from pale Blakean nightgowns
      faces of incorruptible innocence.
If stones could be milked, these fleeting rivers of melt
      would feed us like flowering trees,
Since Mother Earth, you say, after eons of glacial childbirth
      brings up her whole brood naturally.

But naturally what I want and need and expect is to be loved.
So why, as I grow older, when I lift up my eyes to the hills –
      raw deserts that they are –
Do they comfort me (not always, but sometimes)
      with the pristine beauty of my almost absence?
Not the milk of kindness but the milk of stones
      is food I'm learning to long for.

For Heidi Elrod, Sils-Maria, Graubunden, Switzerland, 2004

NOTES

These poems with birds were written over the fifty years or more I have lived in Britain. Although they bear a close relationship to specific places, they are not arranged chronologically. *North Wales* means that the poem was undertaken and probably completed at Pwllymarch in Cwm Nantcol, Ardudwy (North Wales), which can be seen on the cover of my *Collected Poems 1955–2005* (Bloodaxe Books). Other poems reflect previous connections with Cambridge, Oxford, Hay-on-Wye, Scotland, North Eastern Britain, and the Swiss Alps.

Page 17, 'Bird in Hand': after the cover photograph of Leigh Ann Couch's first book of poems, University of the South, Sewanee, Tennessee.

Page 27, 'Spring Diary': published as part of the sequence 'Ardudwy' in *Astonishment* (Bloodaxe, 2012), set for baritone and piano in 2009 by the Welsh composer Rhian Samuel.

Page 29, 'Carol of the Birds': first published by Kevin Crossley-Holland and Lawrence Sail in their anthology *Light Unlocked: Christmas Card Poems* (Enitharmon Press, 2005).

Page 31, 'Crow Omen': Every year in late autumn an official cull of feral goats takes place around Cwm Nantcol. Professional marksmen locate and kill family groups of nannies and kids, and the corpses are left as carrion.

Page 40, 'Stone Milk': the friable Jurassic limestone (so-named by a friend) that along with ice-melt whitens glacial rivers in the Oberengadin. The Fex Tal is a valley famed for its flowers, which ascends south from three 'Elysian blue' post-glacial lakes.

Grüezi: a dialect greeting in German-speaking Switzerland.

. . . 'smoking torch-like out of Pluto's gloom', from D. H. Lawrence's 'Bavarian Gentians'.

ACKNOWLEDGEMENTS

Both the author and publisher wish to express warm thanks to Neil Astley of Bloodaxe Books for generously giving permission to reprint poems from *Collected Poems 1955–2005* (2005) and from two subsequent collections, *Stone Milk* (2007) and *Astonishment* (2012).

'The Bully Thrush' on pages 34–5 was published in *PN Review* 222, Vol. 41. No. 4 (March–April 2015); 'Winter Idyll from My Back Window', page 38, was published in *Stand* magazine, Volume 13:3 (Autumn 2015).